To my wife and children, who love me in spite of myself

To R. Stephen Ward, my father, who taught me to be helpful

To everyone who suffered question after question as I learned how

And to everyone who patiently waited for me to finish it

This book is dedicated

CONTENTS

The Four Steps of a Sale

FOREWORD

Selling isn't for everyone. But sales is.

Every moment of our lives, we're involved in a transaction—even as a solo party. Sometimes it's that pesky ideomotor process; other times, it's explicitly selling ourselves, the angel on our shoulder, or the devil in our head.

It's my belief that the **process** of the sale is often as influential on the long-term "vibes" of the sale as the product itself. Have you ever thought about what in that sales process made you feel comfortable? Uneasy? Satisfied? Ripped off?

Had the same result occurred, but with a different sales technique, would you still have felt that way?

Too many times, I've experienced "buyer's remorse," and it's often centered around wishing I had gotten the product from someone or somewhere else.

I spent a large part of my early career in automotive, and early in that time, I started working with Ken Ward. Ken and I were both very active members of a specific car forum. His focus was on ICE—an acronym that once meant "in-car entertainment," not today's "internal combustion engine." Confusing acronyms aren't just for SaaS.

Ken never sold on the forum—not even personal items in the classifieds. He wasn't allowed to. The forum had a sponsor that was a direct competitor.

What could Ken do?

Help. Contribute. Build trust. Demonstrate expertise.

Ken made a lot of sales, friends, and even referrals from people who didn't do business with him directly but still recommended him without hesitation. Reflecting on it, I think his next book should be about community-led growth.

In an industry often dominated by hard-sell tactics and high-pressure approaches, Ken stood out. He didn't just sell products; he solved problems. He met customers where they were, listened to their needs, and provided solutions that left them genuinely happy—not just in the moment, but long after the sale was complete.

Of all the wisdom and anecdotes Ken has shared with me over the years, the one that has embedded itself the deepest is:

"You don't have a customer until their second purchase."

As a PLG (product-led growth) practitioner, I know this question-turned-mantra defines the practice. What's old is new.

Regardless of the who, sales is a consultative partnership.

- Are we informing our customer appropriately?
- Are we clear in our offer?
- Do we provide the support post-sale that we imply pre-sale?
- Do we understand what success looks like to all parties?
- Will they want to see us again?
- Could we look them in the eye without shame at renewal?

It can be argued that marketing influences a lot of these answers, and that the product does, and that customer care does—and maybe on paper, they do.

But in the end, the customer is making an agreement with their salesperson. They are holding that individual accountable. That's the name they know, the entry point, the maker of claims, the keeper of promises.

Ken's approach teaches anyone how to be the type of salesperson who can blend a deep understanding of products with the principles of psychology—built on a strong foundation of ethics. Utilizing his method, he and others, including myself, have experienced short sales cycles where both parties—buyer and seller—left the interaction feeling good about what had transpired.

Our deal velocity was created through transparency, expertise, and empathy. Sadly, to many salespeople, this approach feels counterintuitive—that taking time slows velocity; especially when this isn't just empathy toward the needs of a customer, but non-manipulative empathy into how the customer thinks. This wasn't just rare in the auto industry; it was revolutionary across all sales.

At a time when the mantra "I'd rather walk them than have a bad sale" was almost unheard of, Ken was already setting the trend. He didn't just believe in doing right by his customers—he built a methodology around it. That methodology, which has been refined and expanded over the years, is now the heart of this book.

Selling Sustainably is about much more than closing deals. It's about understanding that good sales solve problems and that great salespeople prioritize meeting customers where they are—not forcing them to come to you. The skills and insights in these pages transcend industries, applying to anyone who values integrity, trust, and long-term success in sales.

> You will better understand how to have a happy customer.
>
> You will better understand how to create a champion instead of a detractor.
>
> You will better understand how to create customers often more loyal to you than even the product you represent.
>
> This book couldn't come at a better time. With higher quotas, leaner budgets, and more competition, salespeople are under more pressure to perform, faster, than ever before. It's easy to start relying on batch-and-blast methods, shortcuts, and overdependence on AI. Tools have become less the differentiator in the sales world and more the inhibitor.

Salespeople can now only win by going back to basics. Selling sustainably, being a great salesperson, is the great differentiator.

Across industries, we're seeing a necessary shift toward more sustainable and ethical sales practices. Buyers today are more informed and selective than ever before, demanding transparency, authenticity, and value. Trust has become the currency of sales, and short-term wins are being replaced by strategies that foster long-term relationships. Ken's methods align seamlessly with this new era of sales, where understanding a customer's journey and meeting their needs is not just preferred—it's expected.

Ken has been at the forefront of this movement for years, and now he's sharing the playbook. Whether you're navigating government contracts, high-value enterprise deals, smaller-scale transactions, or retail counters, the principles in *Selling Sustainably* will show you how to build trust, solve real problems, and create lasting success.

It's been an honor to know Ken for well over two decades witnessing firsthand the difference his principles make.

If you're ready to embrace the future of sales, this book is your guide. Let it transform not only the way you sell but the way you connect with customers on their journey.

Enjoy -

Peter

peterledgrowth.com

PART ONE:

INTRODUCTION

INTRODUCTION

> *"Life is pain, Highness – anyone*
> *who tells you differently is selling something."*
> The Dread Pirate Roberts, *The Princess Bride*

Selling is a dirty word to many of us.

When many of us think of "selling," we think of deception, manipulation, and "high-pressure tactics" – and as a result, we stay as far away from selling as we can.

We may have been told since we were kids to watch out for salespeople – that they will lie to us, cheat us, and take advantage of us. Maybe we've actually been victims of such people. As the movie quote above shows, this stereotype is even a part of our popular culture.

That's why some people avoid sales jobs – or, we avoid the "selling" part of our jobs – because we think it requires us to jettison our scruples to achieve results. Some even think that performance-based commission pay plans cause unethical behavior.

Does selling force us to be unscrupulous?

No – it is possible to sell ethically, honestly, and effectively. It's also possible to sell respectfully – without pressure or manipulation. This book is filled with tools and techniques to help you do that.. The principles involved may be from the retail floor, but they are about people and how we make decisions – so they are applicable in any field where results depend on convincing others to come with you. These tools and techniques are "The 12 Keys of Selling."

The 12 Keys of Selling fall into three parts:

The Rules are about the ethics of selling - helping us stay ethically grounded, personally engaged, and professionally effective.

The Patterns are about Relationships. The Pattern Map is a tool to help us know ourselves better, so we can consciously shift our mode of operation to what works best for each person and the Pattern they are using. We discuss four basic Patterns.

The Steps describe the process of a sale - guiding us through it, explaining what happens and when it happens, and how to follow a sequence which prevents "high-pressure" situations.

Why does selling exist?

Selling as a process exists because people make decisions in confusing , counterintuitive ways – not always choosing a good product on its merits, and not always avoiding a bad product on its shortcomings. Evaluating products is difficult.

VHS outlived the technically superior Betamax, the touchscreen Newton failed long before the iPhone succeeded, and so on. Most products aren't an iPhone, taking over a category with such dominance that several existing handset players went out of business. Most products exist alongside competitors, with advantages and disadvantages, and the products your company offers need advocates.

Some believe sales is getting people to do what you want them to do, but this is a short-sighted definition. Selling at its best is, at its heart, a service. It requires quickly deciding what facts are important to each customer and highlighting those facts – but it's also deciding how to present those facts in a manner that works for each individual customer, without pressing anybody's buttons. Here's an example.

The famous 1950's comedy team Abbott and Costello had a bit called the "Susquehanna Hat Company." In it, Costello asked each passerby, one after another, how to find the Susquehanna Hat Company – and each person in turn flew into a rage due to some unlikely and obscure connection between the hatmaker and some recent tragedy in their lives. This is analogous to how sales presentations go – you can step on a land mine of a topic without realizing it. In the skit, Costello couldn't have known that the mention of the Susquehanna Hat Company would trigger such emotional and irrational responses – but in sales, we can often make some quick decisions that can help keep us from triggering similar emotional reactions.

This isn't manipulation – it is giving the customer, our company, and our product offering a fair shake.

I've worked in telephone sales, as a carpet cleaner selling add-ons, on sales floors of consumer electronics stores, in B-to-C sales direct to consumers over email using leads generated by a website, and in account sales management to both small business accounts and key national accounts.

I learned something early on – whatever a sales "natural" is, I'm not one. Frankly, one of the key traits of being a "natural" is personal charisma - which rarely goes hand-in-hand with subject-matter expertise or project management skills. Another seems to be what this layperson would call sociopathy (if you're a sociopath, please stop reading now – this isn't the kind of help you need). Many "naturals" need this book as much as anyone, so they can be well-rounded team members who consistently add value.

The only reason I've been successful in sales (in those places and times that I have been successful) is because I've followed these precepts, consciously or not. In retrospect, when I've been unsuccessful, even if I was following all of the Four Steps, I wasn't following all Four Rules, or I wasn't aware of my Pattern and how it was interacting with the client's Pattern.

These concepts have helped me ethically and effectively sell to my customers. That's helped me in several jobs – sales jobs and otherwise – as well as in several business ventures. Currently, I manage technical marketing for an international consumer electronics company, and I manage two communities for consumer electronics professionals in certain sales and technical fields – but I still use these 12 keys almost every day.

The toughest sale I ever made was enrolling a VP of Finance into authorizing a large-scale test of a product plan. This particular executive preferred data and analytics over forming relationships at work; he had a reputation for being change averse. The proposed plan might have lost 20 percent of the gross profit generated by our top-selling model, or it might have improved unit sales enough to reverse a 5-year decline. That one-on-one meeting took almost every principle in this book to complete, and it was a success (so was the plan – we reinvigorated the sales of that model for years). Later, I was the head of product and sales for a start-up, and I couldn't have done that job without these concepts.

To be successful in sales, you don't have to be a natural – but you can use a good blueprint to follow. This book can help small business owners, sales engineers, account managers, and retail salespeople selling anything from cameras to kayaks to software to services – if they want to do so ethically and effectively. That's where the "Sustainably" comes from - this is all about creating and sustaining long-term commercial relationships. This is a great blueprint to follow – would you like to give it a go? Read on.

THE FOUR RULES

L ook, I hate rules (at least *someone else's* rules), and I know I'm not the only one. For that reason, I've kept the Four Rules as simple and as minimal as possible. If you hate rules as much as I do, do me a favor and give this section a chance *before* you make up your mind.

In sales, if we don't earn business, we fail. That leads some to cross ethical lines, and others to never take the first step. The Rules give us a framework to keep us grounded. The Four Rules may seem so obvious as to not need discussion – but let's take a moment and do just that.

I've met many smart people with a bias against sales jobs, convinced that sales work requires unethical behavior. I don't believe that is true. It turns out I've been able to follow The Four Rules in my sales career. I won't pretend I always understood them, and I won't pretend I haven't "missed the mark" at times in my life, but my life and my career would have benefited if I'd done an even better job following The Four Rules.

RULE ONE: ALWAYS TELL THE TRUTH

When I was a kid, I thought about becoming a lawyer. I didn't know any lawyers, and I didn't know much about lawyers – but I thought I did! I thought to be a lawyer, you had to lie – so I decided against a career in law.

Now, as an adult, I know I was wrong. Lawyers don't have to lie to do their jobs (although some of them seem to offer it as a free service).

The same misconception exists about sales - lying isn't required. Some salespeople do lie, but again, it's optional. This is more of a comment on human imperfection in situations involving financial reward than a statement on selling itself. Just like in life, some people do lie – *but we don't have to.*

The excellent 1996 film Fargo uses a classic stereotype of a salesperson; William H. Macy's character was, in the words of one of his customers, "A %^$& liar!" But simply having a sales job doesn't make someone a liar – it only gives liars a place to happen. They can happen anywhere.

Don't fool yourself into thinking that sales is the only line of work with ethical challenges. We've heard of accountants fudging numbers, entrepreneurs making up positive test results, and engineers lying on their diesel emissions reports – ethical pressures can appear in any business when the leadership is poor.

We can be successful in sales without lying. It requires us to be strong enough to not take the easy way out when we're on the spot. It is easier if we exercise caution about the company and boss we work for. It's easiest if we are confident that the product is competitive. The worst lies are always ones that we tell ourselves.

Most of us are lousy liars, so our would-be clients know at some level when we are lying to them. Sales works better when we take every advantage we can, and lying is a lousy way to convince anyone of anything.

Rule One has a powerful side effect – the confidence that comes from knowing we're telling the truth makes us more convincing.

RULE TWO: SERVE EVERYBODY

Rule Two, Serve Everybody can be interpreted a couple of ways, but at its core this Rule is about a commitment to adding value.

- *Help everyone who comes your way.* I've seen salespeople in car stereo shops assume that a bicyclist doesn't have a car – and so they then assume that person was not a qualified customer. I've seen companies use internal sales processes that lead to ghosting potential customers. Don't make that mistake. Perhaps the only service you will be able to offer is directions – put yourself in a position to offer that service, and if that is all you get to do, you will create goodwill through helping someone else. That's always a good thing to do.

- *Do your best to help everyone* – help even if helping them forces you out of your comfort zone. In rare cases, this includes finding another available salesperson to help the client if you decide you're not being effective.

- *Be aware of your unique responsibilities.* On one hand, you represent your employer, your teammates, and your suppliers (the companies that make the products you offer). On the other hand, you have a responsibility to the customer. In economics terms, you are at the interface between manufacture and consumption – take it seriously. A lot of people depend on you to do your job ethically and effectively.

Your job is to serve:

- Your potential client
- Your employer
- Your employer's suppliers and partners
- Your coworkers
- Yourself.

You don't help the customer at your company's expense, or the company at the customer's expense, or everyone else at your own expense. You find a path that serves *everyone involved* – your customer, your employer, and you. In some situations, you may fail to find a perfect solution – but you are always looking for one, every time. Today many business scholars teach these ideas under the concepts of "equity."

Your employer may disagree with the above statement, saying, "The only person I want you looking out for is me, and the only company you should be looking out for is this company." Believe it or not, I've seen business owners and managers with that attitude – and if they own the business or have a sufficient amount of responsibility in the business, they have the right to decide what they want their employee's priorities to be.

Rule Two isn't optional for me, it's a core part of my world view. This is how I live my life regardless of what my boss thinks – or the business owner, or anyone else. If our boss is so afraid of loss – and so zero-sum oriented and survival-based in their thinking to attempt to require me to take this sort of approach – then we may need to get a new job. (Before I do, I need to make sure my boss has a bite that is as bad as his bark. Many old-school bosses will talk mean and tough, but few of them will actually follow through punitively against an ethical employee who gets the job done.)

RULE THREE: COME TO PLAY EVERY DAY

*"I'm not even supposed to **be** here today!"*
Dante, Clerks (1994)

Actually – as his friend Russell explains to him – Dante went to work that day of his own free will; he just liked playing victim to his job.

Many of us take Dante's approach to work. Letting work happen to us, going through the motions, and waiting for the weekend. The 12 Keys system won't work as well when that's your approach. This system requires you to *choose* to come into work every day and to *choose* to make a positive impact on the people you work with. This book can teach you responsible, ethical selling, but it won't teach you how to care – that's a choice you have to make yourself.

The 12 Keys system works when we take responsibility to become more effective with all kinds of people – and taking responsibility means we shift our mode of operation to heighten our effectiveness. We don't compromise our authenticity, and we certainly don't pretend to be someone we aren't – but we act with compassion.

Some of us want to be recognized for who we are, without artifice or facade. I think that's probably a universal human trait, but I also know it's stronger for some of us than others. It's funny – after decades, I have had regular customers share with me why they enjoyed our interactions, and they were for those qualities I have always hoped people notice. They will see who you are – it's really hard to hide who we are. You just need to get out of the way, so they can see clearly.

This Rule has a hint of double-dipping in it, in that I used the word "play" very specifically. This isn't my book about brain surgery – it's sales, and the stakes are not life or death. No one has a 100 percent success rate in sales – like in baseball, a good percentage isn't close to 100 percent. Emotionally, this is important to get our arms around – we can't succeed in sales if our minds are still torturing ourselves about the last at-bat. At the same time, those who succeed are those who practice, look at their mechanics over and over, and treat it like a science (again, just like hitting in baseball). I remember being asked, "How do you deal with the rejection in a sales job?" Well, I was raised in a religious denomination who regularly knocked on their neighbor's doors, attempting to convince them to change religions (and I was terrible at it, by the way). Rejection in sales was a piece of cake compared to interrupting the Game of the Week on Saturday morning to leave a religious tract.

Not all of us have that experience – but all of us have some experience of disappointing rejection. Sales isn't like that, either. No job, no product, and no company with a quality offering fails in sales 100 percent of the time. If you follow these precepts and your percentage is terrible, take a hard look at your offering.

RULE FOUR: MAKE THINGS EASIER

The 12 Keys system is entirely based on making things easier for the client and everyone else we are allied with.

This means:

- Know the answers.
- Know simple, prepared ways to explain those answers.
- Know how to quickly find the answers you don't know.
- Know where to send people to get what you don't offer.
- Understand the commercial environment in which you operate.

Those things are all important, but there is another, deeper level to making things easier. Here's an example. I was working at my first retail sales job in a consumer electronics store. That day, I was running new video cables to all of the televisions in the video area, and I was up on a 10-foot ladder as a result.

An unassuming man came in with his hands in the pockets of his green parka. He quietly started looking around the video section. I was right in the middle of a very tricky bit of cable routing, and so I greeted him as I worked – still on top of the ladder. I said hi, apologized for the mess, and asked how I could help him out. He replied that he was "just looking." "Great," I replied, "What can I point you toward?" He started asking me questions about VCRs, I answered a few of them, and as I finished a cable connection, I started down the ladder.

Fortunately, I was paying attention. When I got halfway down the ladder, I think the customer realized that he would soon be my sole focus of attention. This didn't seem to be a positive realization for him. He reminded me that he was "just looking," backed six feet away, and started looking down at his shoes – he was *nervous*.

My response wasn't very well reasoned, but it turned out to be right. I immediately went back up the ladder and grabbed those coaxial cables. I saw the customer take a few steps forward, back to where he had been standing, and our conversation continued where it had left off.

A few minutes later, I had answered all of his questions, determined the model he turned out to be interested in fit his budget *and* was in stock, and voluntarily explained our return and price protection policies. Everything pointed toward writing up the sale – the only problem was, I was still on top of that ladder. How could I get down off the ladder without scaring my customer? Simple – I asked his permission. "Would you like me to go in the back and get one of those for you?" He said yes – and *then* I came down.

During that conversation – that *sale* – I routed the same video cables to the same TV half a dozen times. Was this disingenuous on my part? Maybe a little. I think that my customer was so resistant to the idea of talking to a salesperson, anything more direct would have failed – he would have bailed out of the conversation. I know that he got a great product at a fair price and that my help was the reason why (he picked out a VCR from the number one manufacturer at the time in reliability according to the nation's leading consumer magazine). *If I had made getting down off of that ladder more important than my customer's sensitivities, he probably wouldn't have become a customer.*

This is making things easier at a deeper level. At this level, making things easier requires you to conduct yourself in such a way that your message has the best chance of getting a fair hearing. It's a desire to provide true service. Don't "spin" your recommendation, and don't break the First Rule. Just avoid running into a ditch by accidentally "pressing someone's buttons." It's by making things easier that we can become most effective – in sales, in business, and in life.

USING THE RULES

The Four Rules:

1. Always Tell the Truth.
2. Serve Everybody.
3. Come to Play Every Day.
4. Make Things Easier.

Looking at these rules spelled out like like this, they may seem overly simple – but that's not because they don't work. Some of us prefer complexity! Some folks seem to think success at anything must require a complex process – but maybe, if it can be arrived at using simple principles, we lose our excuse for not having succeeded yet?

On the other hand, I've met so many people who fear sales positions because they are convinced of the innate need to violate precepts like these four. I absolutely guarantee that it's possible to be a successful salesperson while following The Four Rules. If you're in an environment where you're asked to break the Four Rules, that's an artifact of the culture and the leadership – and believe me, that will impact everyone in the company, not just the salespeople.

When these simple principles don't work, it's usually because we aren't using them. Wouldn't everyone's lives be better if they followed these four basic ideas?

PART TWO:

THE PATTERN MAP

THE MYTH OF THE RATIONAL ACTOR

When I applied for my first retail sales job, I explained to the interviewer that I had a plan to avoid any unscrupulous high-pressure tactics. I would simply learn all there was to learn about the products we were selling, offer this information to every would-be customer – and then the customer would make a rational decision based on the information I'd supplied.

The interviewer laughed, but for some reason he hired me anyway. It turns out there was a tent sale coming up, and they needed green hires to work the event – and I did do well enough to not have to go back into construction!

The process I described – the buyer rationally evaluating all the pertinent data and making a decision – turns out to have a name. *It's called the "rational actor model."* It presumes that we can determine all of the factors a person will use to make a decision, and we can predict what decision that person will reach, using a rational analysis of that person's self-interest as our guide.

The "rational actor model" presumes that emotion is not part of our decision-making process.

However, as it turns out, the rational actor is a myth, or a fictional character – Spock from *Star Trek* is the classic example. He's a classic character - but Vulcans aren't real.

Scientists have found that people make decisions at a deep, unconscious level, with emotion as a component of our decisions– and our rational minds often make up seemingly logical explanations for our decisions after the fact. *Emotions are the essence of what spurs us to take action.*

It also turns out that our emotions are an essential part of successful decision-making. People who suffer from localized brain injuries that have impacted their emotional capabilities also lose their ability to make good decisions – even when their rational, cognitive faculties are unharmed! (For more on this subject, see the story of Phineas Gage in Antonio Damasio's book *Descartes' Error.*)

Emotions aren't just part of how we reach *good* decisions – they are also, of course, part of how we reach *bad* decisions. Our emotions power the unconscious defense mechanisms that protect us from the world. Bad decisions can make it past the alarm system, it's true.

Sometimes, these mechanisms are triggered by a false alarm. If we are in the middle of a decision, and a defense mechanism is triggered, it will often bring the process to a screeching halt – whether the trigger was for a good reason or not. Part of professional sales is to avoid triggering those false alarms. Part of being a decent human being is not being the reason these alarms exist in the first place (hence, the Four Rules).

THE "PSYCH 101 MISTAKE"

The "Psych 101 Mistake" is when a student is first introduced to the study of human behavior – and immediately spends their time loudly analyzing and explaining the behavior of everyone around them (unbidden, of course). They may get it right, and they may not – but either way, they are a royal pain in the neck.

Don't make the Psych 101 Mistake. For example, don't take this Pattern Map that we're giving you for a specific purpose – interacting with customers – and start using it constantly to explain (out loud) the behavior of everyone you know. Also, don't make the mistake of deciding that the pattern someone is using is anything more than that – *a **tool** they are using*. This is not a personality test – it's not sophisticated enough, or in-depth enough, for that. It is a decision-making-style model. It may certainly help you when interacting with other people – I hope that it does – but don't go overboard, please. The Pattern Map model is a tool, just like a pencil sharpener is a tool – don't sit there and turn the crank for no good reason.

Before you start with everyone else, look inward.

THE PATTERN MAP CONCEPT

What the Pattern Map is — and what it isn't

When I first came to Portland, Oregon, I visited Powell's Books, where I found a Walking Map of Portland. (Powell's gives them away!)

It fit in my pocket. It showed all the downtown streets. That map was great! I used it as I walked all over town — through the Park Blocks, the waterfront, and the museums. I had a great time.

The next day, I used it to plan a route to take while driving my car. This time, the trip was a chaotic failure. Do you know why? I ran into some unexpected obstacles: one-way streets and intersections with no left turn.

Why weren't these on my map? Because a Walking Map doesn't have to show them — they don't affect a pedestrian. So, they were left off.

Why did Powell's give out such a poor-quality map? Of course, they didn't give out a poor-quality map — they gave out a Walking Map, which was clearly labeled and very useful for its intended purpose. My problems came from misusing the tool they had provided me.

A map should have enough detail to be useful, but not so much detail that it won't fold up and fit in our pocket. If a map included an accurate description of every bit of the world, it would be the size of the world it describes. Leaving things out is inherent in the creation of any map – it's the most important task!

We're going to give you a very simple map for navigating interactions between people – in real time.

The Pattern Map doesn't capture who we are as unique, special, and complex individuals in the same way that a Walking Map often doesn't show one-way streets. There are dozens of models of human behavior and human "personality," and most of them are incredibly detailed ways of examining something that has happened in the past. Very few are intended to be used "on the fly," like the Pattern Map.

The Pattern model, used properly, will help us follow the Third and Fourth Rules – Help Everyone and Make Things Easier.

When I was taught how to sell, I was taught to treat everyone pretty much in the same way. Over the next 10 years, I got pretty good at my job – but sometimes I failed. My customers and I would sometimes grate on each other rather than "clicking," and I could never figure out why. I did notice that this happened more with people who seemed pretty similar to each other and with some who seemed to have things in common with me – but I never really figured it out completely. I just decided that these "problem customers" were jerks, and I was in the right and they were in the wrong.

Then, I took some classes in communication and effectiveness, and I was exposed for the first time to the idea of "modes" or patterns of human behavior. That's when I started to understand those failures much better. It turns out that using four different patterns to describe human behavior can be traced back to the Greeks and the Hindus - I certainly didn't invent this approach.

"Isn't this like Myers–Briggs?" There are certainly many approaches to analyzing human behavior. The Pattern Map is a tool. It's intended to help you with your task. Many scholarly types have come up

with more complex methods of capturing human behavior – but they are awfully unwieldy to use in real time in a sales interaction. The Pattern Map is not intended to exhaustively categorize every person; it's intended to help us make in-the-moment decisions that help us Serve Everyone and Make Things Easier.

Be very clear – there is no "best" Pattern. We all use all four Patterns at different times – and rightly so. Every one of these four Patterns is optimum for some situations, but not for others. A person who is aware of how they are operating, and can change their behavior to be most effective, creates the best results. If we want to Make Things Easier for ourselves and our clients, we need to learn how to navigate the four Patterns.

DECIDING ON OUR PRIMARY PATTERN

. . . .

The Patterns are descriptions of ways we behave. We usually don't decide consciously what Pattern we will use – it's often an unconscious choice on our part, and most of us tend to use one Pattern more often than the rest.

Before we use the Map to navigate interactions with other people, we need to use it as we look at ourselves and our behavior. Here's the first step of making your own Pattern Map, shown in Figure 1.

STRUCTURED -OR- UNSTRUCTURED?

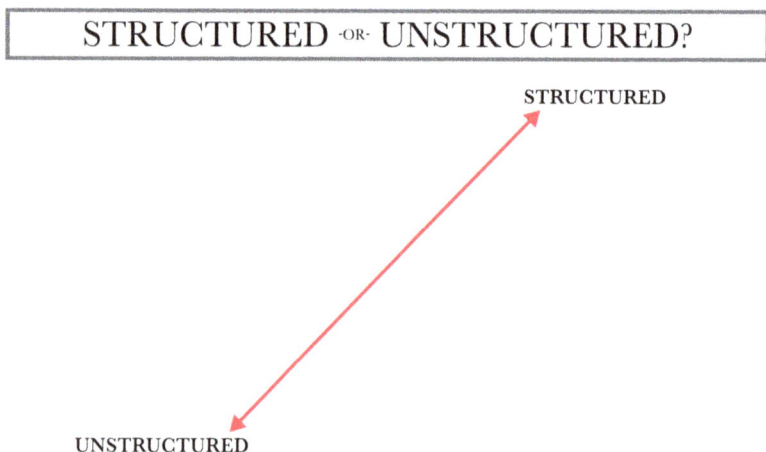

STRUCTURED

UNSTRUCTURED

FIGURE 1

The right end of the spectrum is labeled Structured, and the left end is labeled Unstructured.

Where do we tend to feel more comfortable – in situations that have structure and definition, or in situations that are undefined or loosely defined with room to maneuver? Mark the line on the left or right accordingly, as shown in Figure 2.

STRUCTURED -OR- UNSTRUCTURED?

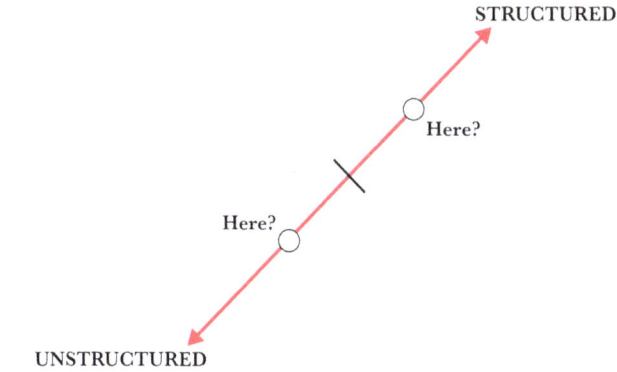

STRUCTURED

Here?

Here?

UNSTRUCTURED

FIGURE 2

ASSERTIVE -OR- ACCOMODATING?

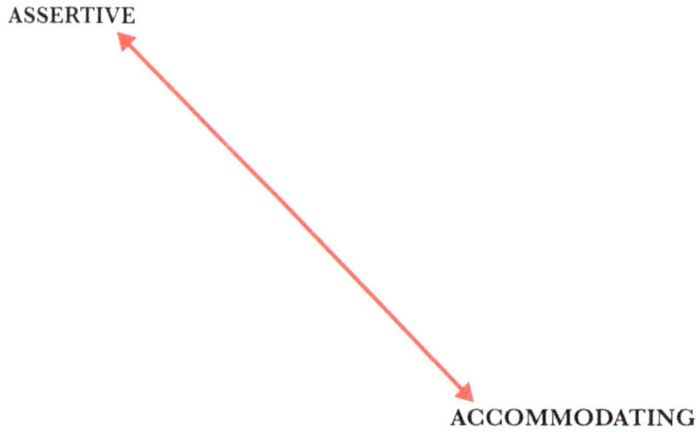

ASSERTIVE

ACCOMMODATING

FIGURE 3

Here's the second step, in Figure 3.

The right end is labeled Accommodating, and the left end is labeled Assertive. Where do you tend to feel more comfortable – when you are asserting yourself in a situation, or when you are accommodating your actions to the situation?

Mark the line accordingly, as shown in Figure 4.

ASSERTIVE -OR- ACCOMODATING?

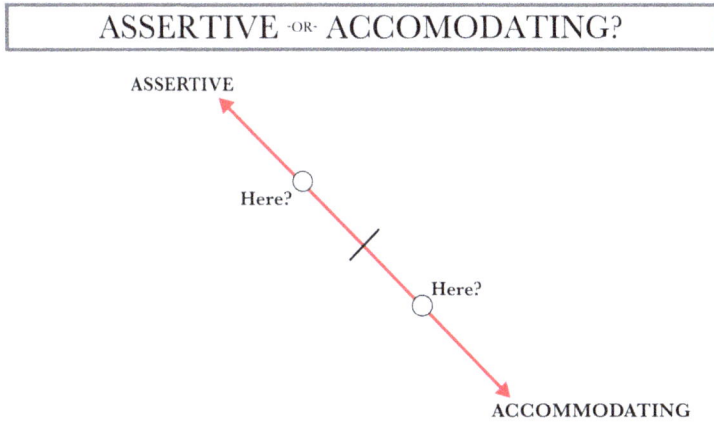

FIGURE 4

NOTE: If you are wondering if you can be perfectly centered on one or both lines, for the purposes of this exercise, mark the sides labeled "Structured" and "Accommodating." We'll talk about this more later.

Now let's combine these two, shown in Figure 5.

THESE TWO TOGETHER MAKE AN "X"

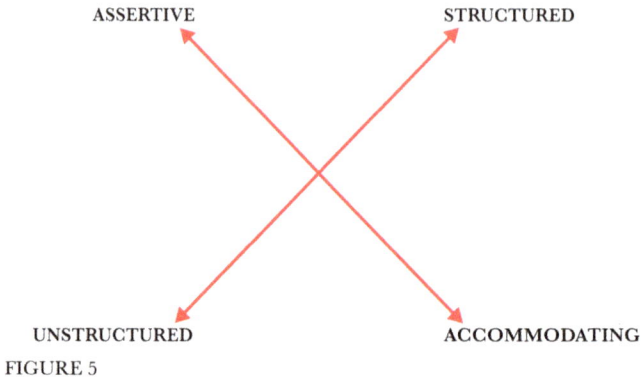

ASSERTIVE   STRUCTURED

UNSTRUCTURED   ACCOMMODATING

FIGURE 5

Mark the quadrant of the circle that matches up to your two ear-lier marks, as shown in Figure 6.

OUR LOCATION ON THE PATH

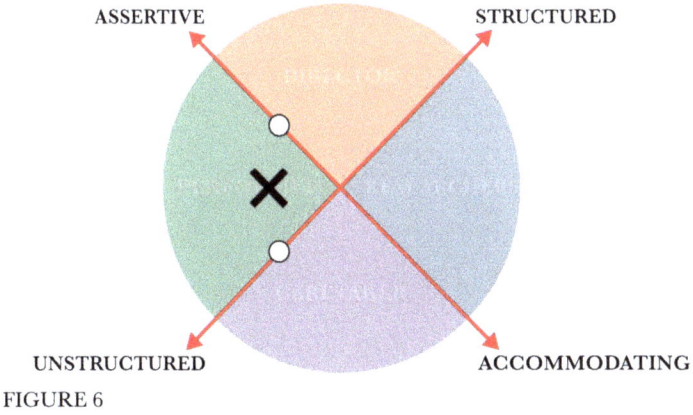

FIGURE 6

Here, we've assigned names to the quadrants – Director, Performer, Researcher, and Caretaker, as shown in Figure 7.

THE FOUR PATTERNS

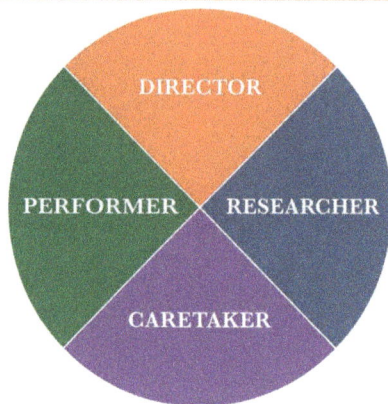

THE PATTERN MAP, LABELED

FIGURE 7

Now, we've put names to these four Patterns.

We haven't found their inner essence, captured their fondest desires, or anything like that – we've just put names on patterns of behavior used to reach decisions.

Now let's add some detail to each of these. For example, we can draw some generalizations regarding making connections (relationships) or focusing on projects (tasks). Many of us lean one way or the other, without realizing it. It's certainly useful to know if a potential customer favors connections with others most highly, or emphasizes the project at hand.

As we do this, you may identify people in your life who use one of these patterns to reach decisions – that is a common reaction. As that happens, remember the Psych 101 Mistake, and keep that concept in your pocket for now.

However, it's very useful to first look at which patterns *you* use to reach decisions.

PERFORMERS

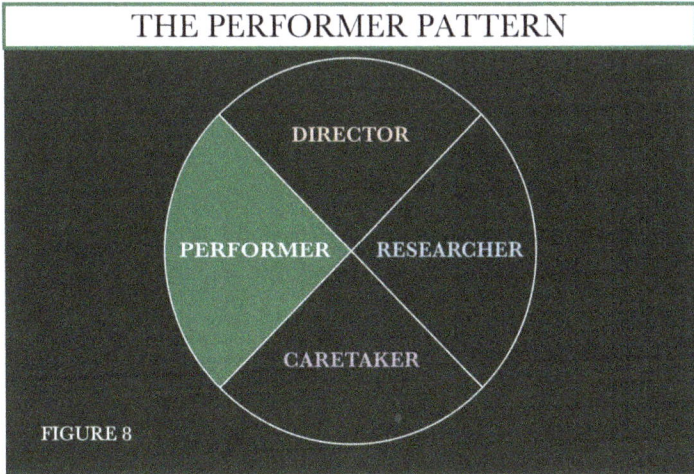

THE PERFORMER PATTERN

DIRECTOR

PERFORMER   RESEARCHER

CARETAKER

FIGURE 8

Those in the Performer quadrant generally avoid rules and boredom, and are often spontaneous and fun. They have a bias toward action, so they have no trouble making a decision, but they often have a relatively short attention span. They are often willing to overspend, so they may return items, or cancel purchases that are priced outside the original budget. That said, sale pricing and discounting is often most effective with Performers.

These folks tend to be more connection-oriented than project-oriented.

Performers are so good at connections with others that some call them "born salespeople." This isn't true, of course – they may be good at human interaction, but they may be terrible at subject-matter expertise or process navigation, and so they may create more problems than they solve.

Performers quickly decide where they want to go to lunch, and they often convince everyone else to go there too.

DIRECTORS

●●●●●●●●●●●●●●●●●●●●●●●●●●●●●●●●●●

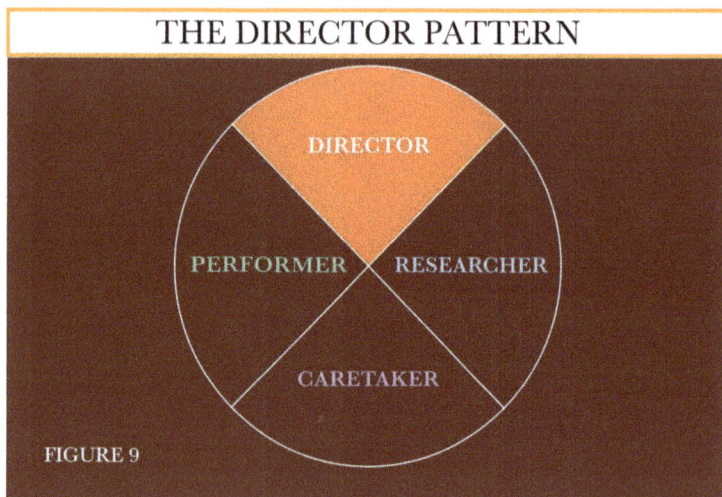

THE DIRECTOR PATTERN

DIRECTOR

PERFORMER   RESEARCHER

CARETAKER

FIGURE 9

The folks using the Director Pattern have a bias toward action, and they are comfortable when they are driving the bus – but they are often uncomfortable if *someone else* is driving the bus. They are very project-oriented and not very connection-oriented. They have no trouble making decisions, but they do it on their own timetable. They gravitate toward positions of responsibility - sometimes openly, and sometimes covertly as untitled gatekeepers. Many are senior executives, and many own their own firms (often small privately held firms without oversight). A Director who works in engineering or accounting will often strive to be an engineering manager or a partner in the firm.

Directors often strive to learn just enough about a category or topic to feel they've identified someone as an expert. Once they have found that trusted expert, they often drop the matter entirely and delegate decisions to that expert. However, this choice may not always be announced out loud – so be ready to pivot!

Directors decide where to go to lunch right away, and announce the decision to the rest of the group.

RESEARCHERS

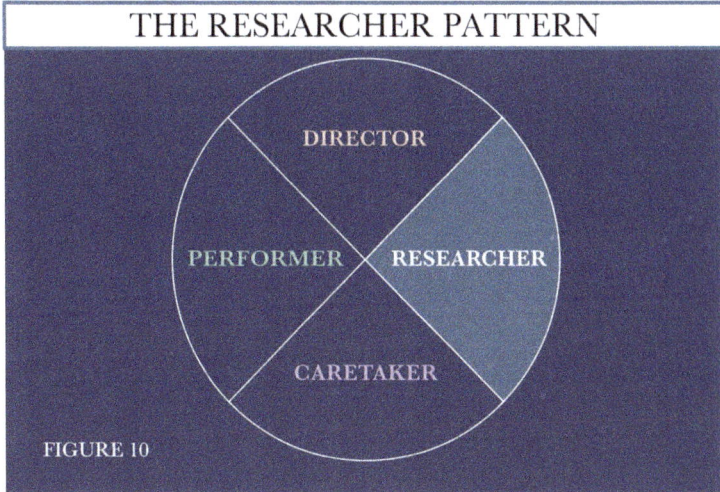

THE RESEARCHER PATTERN

DIRECTOR

PERFORMER   RESEARCHER

CARETAKER

FIGURE 10

Those using the Researcher Pattern love to figure out how things work, and they detest making mistakes – any mistakes. They are comfortable postponing a decision indefinitely, if it means they are avoiding the risk of making a mistake. They won't be pressured – they have years of experience taking their time, so they won't fold just because we try to hurry them along. They are often very project-oriented and not too connection-oriented (but their personal connections are very important to them, and they can be incredibly thoughtful about their loved ones). Researchers often work in complex fields and may not strive for positions of responsibility within those fields – they often enjoy the work and find management distasteful. Many Researchers can be found in engineering, science, medical, and accounting positions.

Researchers can take forever just to decide where to go to lunch, but they often bring data to the problem (e.g., mapping information and online reviews) and share it with the group.

CARETAKERS

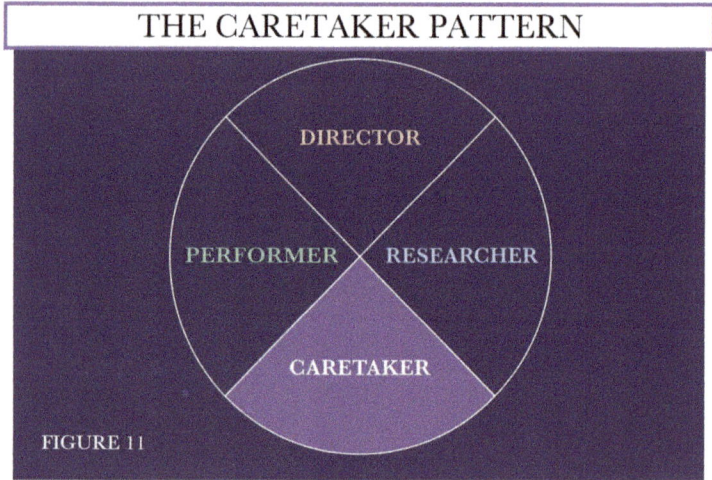

THE CARETAKER PATTERN

DIRECTOR

PERFORMER   RESEARCHER

CARETAKER

FIGURE 11

Those who mainly use the Caretaker Pattern want to see everyone happy and getting along. They are very connection-oriented rather than project-oriented. Identifying their own preferences can be challenging – they are used to going along with what someone else wants when making decisions. Many folks using this Pattern gravitate toward positions where they literally are caretakers – nursing, counseling, teaching, the clergy, and even human resources.

The folks using the Caretaker Pattern often don't realize where *they'd* like to go to lunch, but they are happy when everyone agrees.

OUR PRIMARY PATTERNS WITH CLIENTS

THE PATTERN MAP, LABELED

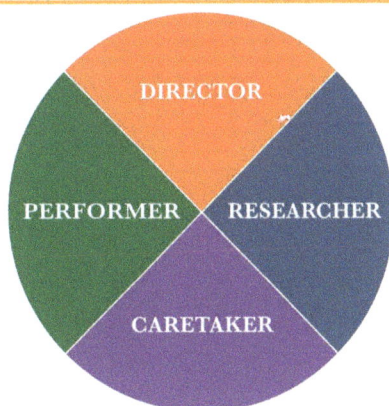

FIGURE 7

If we want to get better results, we need to be very clear about how *we're* operating.

Many people get really excited about using the Pattern Map tool to reduce their clients to a single type, rather than honor them as complex people. Resist this inclination. All of us use every one of these four Patterns at different times, and none of them represent who we are – just some things we do sometimes.

The greatest value from the Pattern Map concept is when we use the Map to look at *ourselves* and how we work with clients. Taking responsibility for our sales interactions, realizing what doesn't work, and changing our course are the marks of a responsible adult and a professional at any vocation. This is especially true when working with B2B sales and selling to groups. The group often contains people who use different patterns, and we can't focus our efforts on just one approach – but if we don't know our own tendencies, how can we tailor our approach for others?

PERFORMERS IN SALES

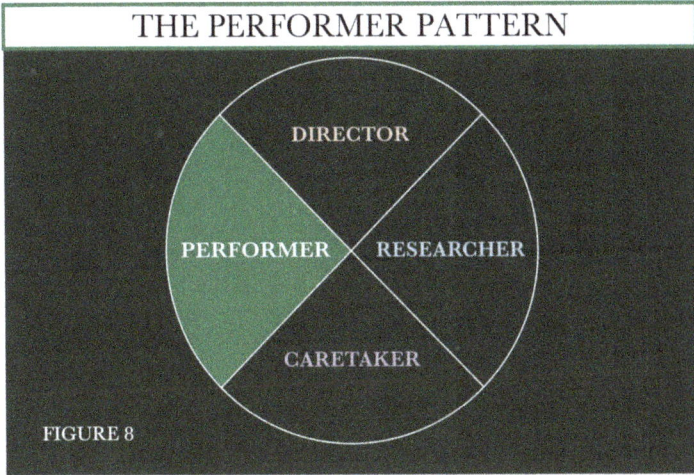

THE PERFORMER PATTERN

DIRECTOR

PERFORMER   RESEARCHER

CARETAKER

FIGURE 8

Performers are often thought of as "natural salespeople" due to their outgoing personalities and willingness to persuade others to take action. Performers may not have a ton of subject-matter expertise or be experts at navigating the company's processes, but they often do a great job when it comes to persuading clients to get happily involved with the company's offerings.

Performers aren't always comfortable with rules and structure, though – they are often more comfortable "winging it." For this reason – especially when working with more complex sales involving a lot of moving parts or staged events – Performers can create that wonderful scenario we call "train wrecks." Train wrecks can take a wonderful commercial opportunity and transform it into a money-losing debacle. It's not enough to seat the party at the table – we have to make sure they get the meal they ordered! We have to stay with the transaction all the way through. (I know that some large companies have split this into separate tasks, and I have my misgivings about such an approach – but most sales jobs require some involvement all the way through.)

Performers benefit most from adding some structure – learning to identify the customer's Pattern and learning the Steps of a purchase process in Part Three (i.e., what happens when). The Four Rules can be a great framework for Performers to use, and the Fourth Step (covered in the next section) is also of crucial importance for Performers to remember.

DIRECTORS IN SALES

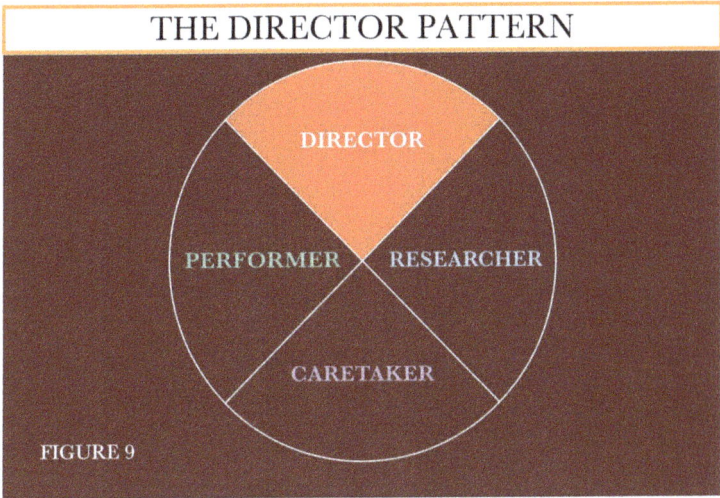

THE DIRECTOR PATTERN

DIRECTOR

PERFORMER RESEARCHER

CARETAKER

FIGURE 9

Directors are comfortable guiding, advising, and counseling customers. That's good. Directors also can overcontrol and micromanage, and they can become very uncomfortable if someone else is in control. This is not so good – especially when the customer is also using the Director Pattern. The interaction can degenerate into an unconscious jockeying for position, neither deferring to the other – and the outcome is rarely a good one. Directors can be very effective using the 12 Keys, as long as they pay attention to their tendencies and reactions and shift when they need to shift.

When Directors are unconsciously reacting to customers, we are often wrestling for control of the discussion – trying to prove who's in charge. This will wreck an interaction with another Director 95 percent of the time (and with Performers a great deal of the time).

I know this because I use the Director Pattern as my Primary Pattern. Until I was conscious of my reactions to other Directors, I lost deals over and over, and of course I blamed the clients for being the problem. Eventually, I realized the common denominator was me.

If you operate using the Director Pattern, and you want to be more effective in sales, I recommend that you make it obvious to others that *they* are the decision-makers − not you. This is crucial with others who also use the Director Pattern. The most important word here is "deference." **Once the sales interaction becomes a jockeying for control, we have lost.**

It's critical that we identify any tendency on our part toward control, command, or "driving the bus" − and we make sure that our interactions with our customers satisfy that desire responsibly. When we're in Director mode, and we fear losing control of the interaction, we may react by trying to grab the wheel, and this doesn't work. The client can always win by simply getting off the bus!

In general, Directors are often clear on their own goals, and they focus on them rather than the goals of their customers. Looking at things from the customer's perspective is an essential part of successful selling.

Once we earn the business, the Fourth Step requires a great deal of bus driving and taking charge − so it's best to be very conscious of how we're operating now, so we can take charge of the project afterward. There will be more on this later.

RESEARCHERS IN SALES

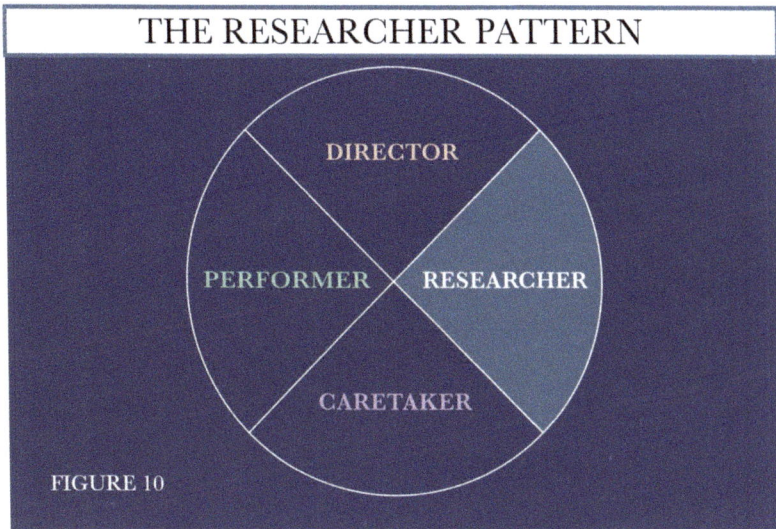

THE RESEARCHER PATTERN

FIGURE 10

Researchers are often uncomfortable approaching customers but are *very* comfortable once the conversation turns to their comfort zone – facts and figures. Researchers know a lot about their specialty – they are generally subject-matter experts – and this can make them incredibly effective at sales. They are also experts at navigating the company's processes (at least the way they are supposed to work – they may not know any of the workarounds)!

They can also be incredibly *ineffective* when they lose track of the objective and share more information than non-Researchers want or need. It's really important to remember that we aren't there to be right; we are there to help people with our company's offerings, and *being right isn't how we keep score*. Researchers are most effective when they carefully select the information to present and when they stay on course throughout the process.

If you're a Researcher in sales, you probably know the subject matter already, and you probably know the company's processes already. What you need to do is learn a sales process to follow – like the Four Steps – and you will be very effective at sales!

CARETAKERS IN SALES

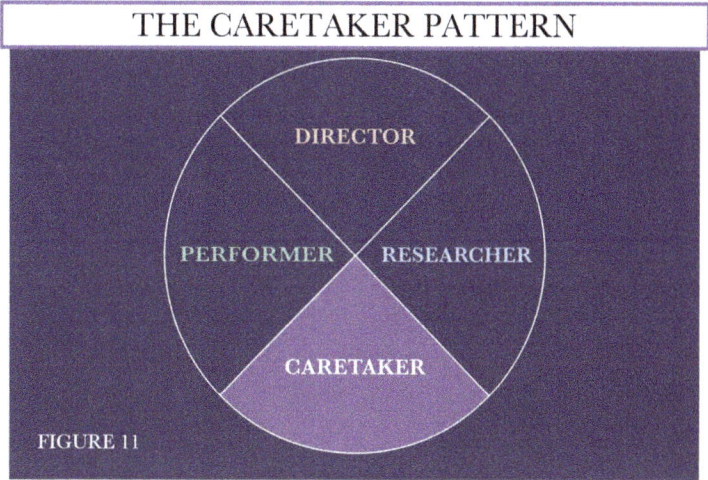

THE CARETAKER PATTERN

DIRECTOR

PERFORMER | RESEARCHER

CARETAKER

FIGURE 11

Caretakers don't want to bother anyone, but they want everyone to be helped. Once Caretakers become clear on how this system is rooted in taking care of customers, they can improve their sales effectiveness remarkably.

Caretakers are often amazingly good at the beginning of the sales process, because they are very comfortable with creating relationships.

They are often uncomfortable with later stages of the sales process, , because they are hesitant to "put someone on the spot." For this reason, as Caretakers read the next section on the Four Steps, pay particular attention to Step Two – the Investigation. Doing a solid job here will give you much more confidence that the solution you've invited them to purchase is the best one available – and that will make you much more comfortable as you wait for them to make their decisions!

WORKING WITH THE PATTERNS AS CLIENTS

• •

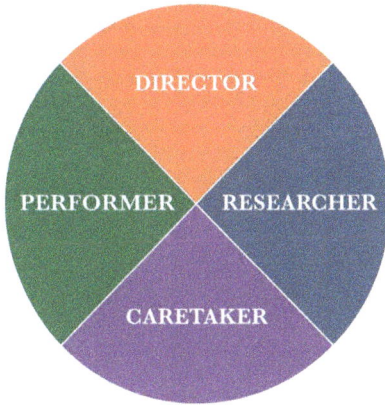

THE PATTERN MAP, LABELED

FIGURE 7

Now, we will discuss dealing with clients who use one of the four Patterns.

Why do you think this section comes *after* the section on the Pattern we tend to use? Because understanding the Pattern the *client* uses is less important than understanding the Pattern *we* use. If we let our preference of Pattern behavior unconsciously guide our client interactions, we could know exactly who we're dealing with, and we still could easily foul up the sale. We could blather on about minutiae, we could be overly controlling, we could skip a step to try to make things faster, or we might ask too much of the client and provide too little expert guidance.

In case that wasn't clear enough, as you read the following pages, see them through the lens of "what we tend to do that *doesn't* add value for these particular clients."

In B2B situations, you're often presenting to a group or committee. In those scenarios, it's helpful to identify the key members and which Pattern each of them is using to make a decision.

WORKING WITH PERFORMERS

**Be fun, avoid data and boring lectures –
be about the experience.**

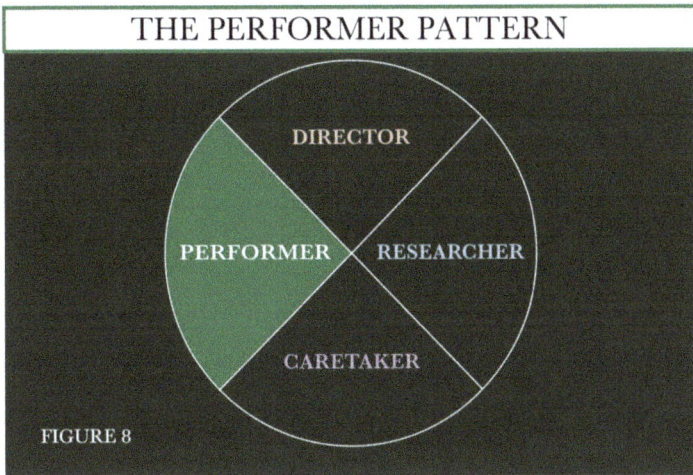

THE PERFORMER PATTERN

DIRECTOR

PERFORMER   RESEARCHER

CARETAKER

FIGURE 8

Performers want to be in the moment and have fun. They do not want to be lectured or drowned in detail, and they do not want to be controlled by others.

Performers don't usually have trouble making decisions unless they involve boring and tedious topics. If you have an attachment to someone buying the right thing for what you think are all the right reasons, you may need to let go of that attachment.

Satisfy the Rule to Serve Everybody by recommending the right solution — but don't try to explain every reason why, or you might bore them to the point where you lose the sale entirely.

WORKING WITH DIRECTORS

Advise and defer — let them drive the bus.

THE DIRECTOR PATTERN

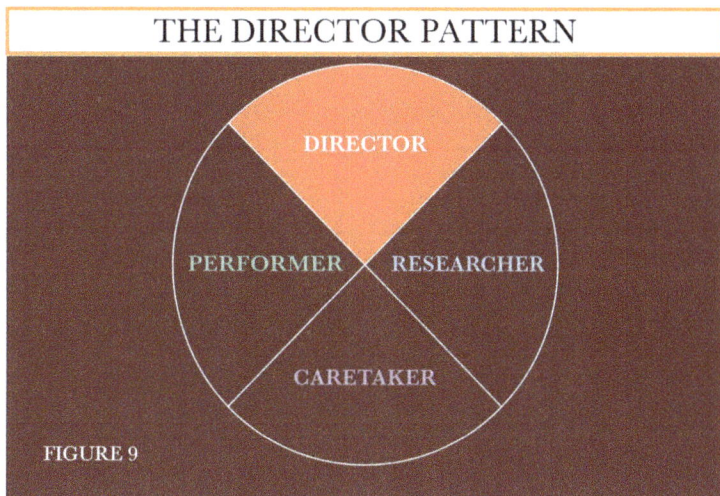

FIGURE 9

A Director customer wants to make a decision and is confident of their ability to do so. They know that they may benefit from your advice, but using you as an advisor is very different from putting you in command of the ship. Directors are often "holding auditions," looking for a company and a person who can augment what they already know. Once they decide you are that person, the audition is over, and they want to move forward – so be ready to make the switch.

Directors like hard data (up to that moment where they make their decision), and they don't care too much about what "most people" have done without specific reasons why (they are often inclined to believe that "most people" are doing it wrong – they'd rather solve problems in a better-than-average way).

They often hold strong opinions. The only hope of success in changing their mind is an excellent explanation, served up free of argumentation or superiority – and the right amount of deference. You can't win an argument with Directors, and it's a mistake to try. Directors don't suffer from "analysis paralysis" – they don't have trouble making up their minds, as a rule. One excellent approach is to ask them for *their* opinions and thoughts – making your advisory position clear and obvious.

When a Director's strong opinion is incorrect and you just have to disagree with it, have a care! This is the riskiest moment with a Director – open contradiction. I have found that what works best for me is being apologetic about having to disagree with them (and believe me, this was *not* my instinctive approach)!

1. Smile with open body language.

2. Soften the statement before you even make it:
   a. "I know it seems odd…"

   b. "This is completely counterintuitive…"

   c. "This surprises a lot of our customers…"

   d. "I hope I explain this correctly, since it may seem a bit backward…"

3. Keep your tone and body language open, and don't react negatively if they don't buy in at first. Making things easier in this case means making your message easier to hear, without knee-jerking reactions.

WORKING WITH RESEARCHERS

Provide data, data, and more data.

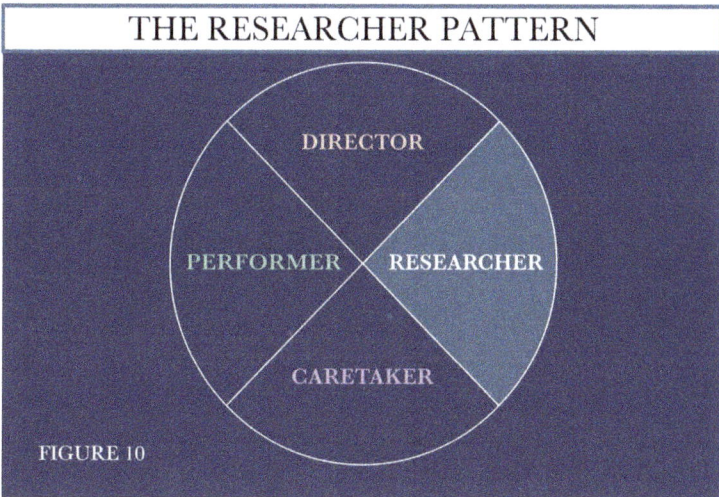

THE RESEARCHER PATTERN

DIRECTOR

PERFORMER   RESEARCHER

CARETAKER

FIGURE 10

Leave and return as needed – nothing that looks like pressure or hurrying.

Researchers can often be identified by their notebooks – they often bring a small notebook and write down pricing and other specifics in it.

Two professions overrepresented in the community of Researchers are accountants and engineers. Both of these professions attract people who place a premium on avoiding mistakes and on following clear rules.

Researchers just don't make decisions as long as there is *any* chance that they might be wrong — they *delay* decisions instead. This means that Researchers aren't easily pressured — it's already been tried for years by their parents, their coworkers, their bosses, and their family members. You're probably not the one who's going to finally crack that shell — so don't try.

Offer all the data you can (if you are new and inexperienced, consider handing a Researcher off to a more knowledgeable staffer). Researchers often say right away, "I'm not buying anything today" — be okay with that, replying, "No problem." I have had success getting their email address — and sending them a detailed proposal with links to external information, pricing, images, and so forth — for them to review at their convenience. This sort of presentation content can often be reused, and it also sets you apart from your competitors. Include early explanations of return and trial policies to lower the perceived risk.

Researchers are seen in brick-and-mortar stores far less often than they used to be. Researchers often shop online, where they think data points are most easily gathered. They may only come into your store to get a chance to touch and feel the product before ordering it online. If you get the feeling that your Researcher customer has a plan like that, I suggest that you make some explanations about your store's customer-friendly policies, and then pleasantly call him on your suspicion. You may be able, with a combination of your return policies and price policies, to overcome the Researcher's inclination toward internet shopping. At least get their email address so you can send them a proposal!

WORKING WITH CARETAKERS

Respect and look out for them as if they were members of your family.

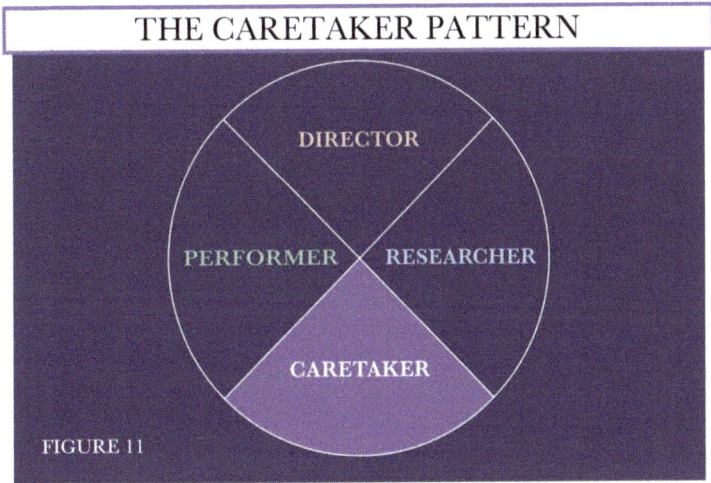

THE CARETAKER PATTERN

DIRECTOR

PERFORMER | RESEARCHER

CARETAKER

FIGURE 11

Caretakers are the easiest people to work with, because they are the only people worried about making sure *you* are happy. For this reason, they are often sold the wrong thing, and they are sometimes taken advantage of. It's important for you to take extra care to set up a Caretaker with the right product, at the right price. If you take advantage, when they come back, they will bring their Director friend or relative to look out for their interests.

In fact, many Caretakers shop with a minder or "ride-along" – who is often a Director and sometimes a Researcher – as the expert who can keep them out of trouble. This sort of combination is also often present in corporate B2B settings – your internal champion may be a Caretaker, and at the same time you have gatekeepers using the Director or Researcher Patterns. A common way to foul this up is to only have one Pattern in mind – when you have multiple stakeholders, take each one's Pattern into account.

USING THE PATTERN MAP

....

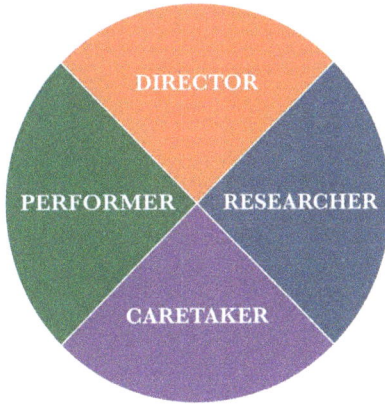

THE PATTERN MAP, LABELED

FIGURE 7

That's a lot of information, so let's boil it down into three principles:

1. **Know yourself.** Know what you're comfortable doing, and accept that your comfort may not be the only criterion for success.

2. **Accept the motivations – conscious or unconscious – of our clients.** Take them into account as we work with the client, and see the humanity in each of them.

3. **Make choices during the sales process that serve everyone.** That means serving the client, your employer, other stakeholders, and yourself.

As you read Part Three – The Four Steps of a Sale – let the Pattern Map inform the choices you make with various clients.

THE FOUR STEPS OF A SALE

INTRODUCTION TO THE FOUR STEPS

When I was starting out, I was taught a nine-step process. I later bought a sales book with *The 7 Steps…* in the title. As a rookie, trying to remember nine steps in order while talking with a potential client was not easy! Seven wasn't much better. After decades of experience, I've defined *my* process with four steps. These Four Steps capture the essence of the purchase decision.

Why is a process important to understand? It's because most stress in a sales interaction – for *everyone* involved – comes from getting the sequence of Steps out of order! Understanding that everyone goes through these Steps in some way helps us respect the client and their process:

- Introduction
- Investigation
- Invitation
- Implementation

During the entire process, the way we communicate is crucial. So, before we discuss these Four Steps, let's cover language and body language.

LANGUAGE

Before we go through the Four Steps, let's talk about language for a moment.

O ur clients are often afraid of being manipulated, deceived, or outmaneuvered. These concerns are understandable, so let's not make them worse! Our clients have incredible amounts of agency and self-direction – they are often the final arbiters of whether or not a purchase happens – and it's beneficial for everyone to emphasize this fact.

Phrases to Avoid

These phrases don't emphasize the agency the client has, and they have a connotation of being trapped or stuck:

- Sign the contract
- Pay
- Sign here
- Buy
- How did you want to pay?

Phrases to Use

These phrases emphasize the agency of the client, and they remind everyone involved that the client is in charge:

- Approve the paperwork
- Take care of the total, handle the balance
- Give us your okay here
- Own
- How would you like to take care of it?

I've had some people object to the above list, saying that using euphemisms like these are intellectually dishonest. Okay – let's look at that idea. Do you really think that your customer in this situation would be unaware that they are buying something? Do you think I am suggesting that you not tell the customer when they are signing a contract? No – of course not.

I do believe that terms like "sign the contract," "pay," and "sign here" have negative connotations for many people in our society, and they can bring up fears or negative past associations in the customer's mind that are unrelated to the current situation. If I know that I've been honest and that the product I'm recommending is a good one, I have no concerns about choosing terms that may have less emotional baggage attached to them.

Types of Questions

Closed-Ended Questions:

- Can I help you?
- Can I help you find something?
- Can I help you, or were you just looking?
- Anything we can help you out with today?

Open-Ended Questions:

- What can I help you find?
- What can I point you toward?
- How can I help?
- What were you looking for?
- What do you think of this?

BODY LANGUAGE

. . . .

Just as we just took a moment to discuss language, **let's take another moment to discuss body language.**

The most important use of body language in retail is to avoid sending negative signals to our clients.

"Closed" body language indicates defensiveness, distrust, and guardedness. "Open" body language indicates a willingness to be vulnerable, trust, and general openness. These signals are usually unconscious – we all pick up on these signals without realizing it.

If we cross our arms, our customers will often cross their arms. This heightens their defensiveness, and so it violates the Fourth Rule – Make Things Easier. If we know that we're not going to lie or deceive, we shouldn't provide any kind of motivation to our customers to distrust us. It isn't reasonable.

The second most important use of body language is interpreting the language our customer is using. Initially, during the Introduction, we often will see closed body language from our customers. During the Investigation, we may see some softening of that stance. During the recommendation, if we see some closed body positions reappear, we know that we may have some more explanation or Investigation to do. If we see a change to open body language during the recommendation, that's a powerful sign that our customer is comfortable with what they are hearing.

Closed Signals:

- Crossed arms
- Hands in pockets
- Arms across front with hands joined
- Crossed legs or ankles
- Arms behind backStanding behind a counter
- Seated behind a desk
- Clenched hands
- Leaning against somethingConstant glances away

Open Signals:

- Arms hanging at sides
- Hands relaxed on hips
- Legs uncrossed
- Eye contact
- Standing in the open, away from desks or counters

STEP ONE: THE INTRODUCTION

The ideal Introduction should provide real evidence of why you – and your company – are trustworthy.

This is how the person is introduced to your business – and to you. The Introduction is over in a few moments, and much of what creates the first impression is already done (or undone) before you ever see the customer.

Most of the Introduction isn't based on what you say - it's your advertising, your website, your social media, your front door and parking lot, and your body language, your demeanor, and how you present yourself. We used to judge people by "professional appearance," and it didn't work well. Now, we're often judged by authenticity.

If there is bad word of mouth, a low-quality website or social media presence, a dirty parking lot, or a store looking unkempt *before* the customer arrives, it's too late to do anything about it *after* the customer arrives. It's said that luck is where preparation meets opportunity. Here, the opportunity is the customer contacting the business – have you done your preparation?

In retail, the tasks of cleaning glass, vacuuming, and housekeeping are similar to the task of sweeping the dojo for a karate student; it is a never-ending process. In virtual communication, we often don't have control over the website, the social media properties, the consumer review apps, or the expert review sites – what the potential client has been exposed to before they meet us. However, knowing all those things – or knowing the client's mind and what they're likely to have seen and read – is another way to sweep the dojo.

During the Introduction, it's important to be genuinely friendly (without being forced) and to avoid closed-end, "say-no" questions. Pay close attention to body language, choice of words, and facial expressions – starting with your own. This is true even if we are communicating without a visual component – even if the client can't see us. Our body language impacts us as much as it does others (more on this in a bit).

STEP TWO: THE INVESTIGATION

The purpose of the Investigation is to determine what the client's problem is, and how it can be solved.

This is when you ask questions so that you can learn more about the customer's needs – more than the customer knows! The best mindset for the Investigation is that the client doesn't know exactly how to solve the problem – because if they did, the problem would already have been solved.

Law & Order was a famous TV show – one that almost single-handedly created the category of "police procedural." On *Law & Order*, did the detectives go around asking, "Who killed the victim?" No, they didn't. If everybody knew who killed the victim, the detectives would be out of a job! Instead, they ask questions to learn about the situation, they form a theory, and they test the theory.

Approach the Investigation as if you were a detective, and you're trying to solve the mystery by talking to someone who knows all of the answers – *but who doesn't know that they know all of the answers.*

Avoid questions that presume a basic level of knowledge. There's no reason for the customer to know any of your jargon, or to spend time studying your specialty. Some seem to think that the consumer is already an expert! Look, if they were an expert, they would order from an online retailer, or build their solution themselves and not even contact you or come into your store. Make sure you don't accidentally make them feel dumb by assuming knowledge they don't have.

During these first two stages, you'll be deciding what Pattern the customer is using from the Pattern Map. This requires you to pay attention to nonverbal cues – remember, body language and facial expressions are where most of our communication happens.

- Does the customer want to be in charge of the process?
- Does the customer have a notebook, browser printouts, or a lot of questions?
- Does the customer get bored quickly?
- Does the customer seem very amenable and trusting?

The answers to these questions will be helpful in Part Three.

STEP THREE: THE INVITATION

· ·

The purpose of the Invitation is to propose a solution and then modify the proposal as needed to earn the business.

This is the step we begin after we've collected enough information – we recommend a solution and invite the customer to purchase it. I call this section the Invitation because it's not enough to recommend the right product – we have to remember to ask the customer to purchase it and do so in a way that is tailored for them.

Before you can do that responsibly, you have to gather enough information about what the customer's looking for, and you have to determine which decision Pattern they are using.

When you make your Invitation, present it appropriately for the Pattern that the customer is using.

I recommend that you prepare a list of values for buying from your store and prepare all of your explanations with this concept in mind. Rather than telling clients what your values are, embody them in your message.

After you make the Invitation, there is usually a discussion about it and perhaps objections – this is perfectly normal. If you learn more or change your mind during the discussion, you may decide to change your recommendation and invite them to buy something else instead.

When making any recommendation, *always explain the value*.

Many salespeople read the feature lists – you know, the bullets on the side of the box or the product website – to clients. This is both insulting to clients (at least those who are literate and have average eyesight) and misses the point. Each feature has a reason for existing, but few of those reasons are obvious, and few of them are equally valuable to everyone.

So, explain the value, not the feature itself.

Exercise:

- Pick your favorite product in your line at the moment.

- List ten aspects of the product and the value of each. (If ten seems like too many, this is an excellent exercise for you.) For example:

  "The fully-regulated power supply keeps the amplifier at top performance regardless of the electrical load – for instance, at night when your car's headlights are on, your amp will still make full power and sound great. Unregulated power supplies lose watts as the voltage decreases, even slightly."

- Now decide which values on the list will appeal to people using the four different Patterns.

Here are some example questions which invite the customer to make the purchase:

"So is this what you'd like to do?

How would you like to handle the deposit?

So, have we covered everything?

Ready to handle the paperwork?"

After you ask this question, shut up. They may need to take a moment to think. Interrupting this because you're nervous or apprehensive is making this moment - which should be about the customer - about you instead. Resist that temptation. Shut up.

OBJECTIONS ARE QUESTIONS IN DISGUISE

So, when you Invite someone to make a decision, you essentially have three possible responses:

- **Yes**, let's do it
- **No**, followed by a conclusive end to the conversation (they leave, ask you to leave, hang up, etc.)
- A reason why the client doesn't want to agree **yet**

It's really important to start any conversation about objections with a congratulatory message to you, the salesperson. Well done! You created enough of a relationship early on – in the Introduction and the Investigation – where the potential client felt safe sharing this problem with you rather than walking out.

Now, you just have to determine how to deal with the objection. If the objection is based on a realization that the product won't solve the client's problem, and you agree that it won't solve the client's problem, then pushing beyond this point breaks the First and Second Rules. That's how you lose clients and increase your own stress. You're presenting the wrong solution.

Still, most of the time, an objection is the result of us extending the Invitation a bit too early – there are some points the client is unclear about. We may have known about these points already, or they may be additional information. If they are new to us, it's important that any reaction to them be muted. *We don't want the client to feel as if they're doing this wrong* – we're the professionals, not them! Take responsibility for your communication, whether it be incomplete or misunderstood.

So, when a client raises an objection, do three things:

1. **Smile!** They just trusted you with valuable information about their current feelings. Be grateful and appreciative.
2. **Thank them** and establish commonality.
   a. "Thanks for letting me know about that, I can see how I would want that sorted out if I were in your shoes."

   b. "Thanks for sharing your concern with me, let's explore that for a moment to make sure I understand correctly."

   c. "Yes, I can see how that would be a big deal."

3. **WADE in!**

I use the WADE formula for dealing with objections:

- **W**hy is that a problem, exactly?
- **A**gree and accept
- **D**isagree and deny
- **E**xplain better

Why is that a problem? Because if we don't understand the objection, this is the proper response. Once you do understand it, one of the three responses below will be the proper one.

Agree when the objection is based in fact, but you don't think it is insurmountable. These are often based on price and value.

Disagree when the objection is not based in fact and doesn't require much explanation. These are often based on an incomplete understanding of your offering. Disagreement must be done kindly and with respect, and it must be preceded by the Smile and Thanks steps above!

Explain when the objection is based on a misunderstanding, often due to our incomplete presentation or the client's misunderstanding of the problem. I start out my explanation with some form of saying, "Yes, I can see how that would be a problem. Fortunately, that turns out not to be the case, and I apologize for not explaining that more clearly earlier."

After you've handled an objection using one of the four options above, I recommend mentioning one more positive value of your offering before returning to your Invitation. I want the last item discussed with my client to have been a positive truth about my recommendation – not a negative misunderstanding. Support your client in making a decision from a position of optimism rather than worry or concern.

INVITING PERFORMERS

Performers don't have trouble deciding. Performers may decide more quickly than you expect them to. With these customers, you need to be flexible, as they may decide without enough information.

Don't drag them through your decision process! If you make the purchase process boring and drawn out, that's how you'll lose them! At the same time, you have to make sure they buy the right thing for them – don't abdicate responsibility just because they are ready to spend money. Be nimble and "flow-with," and you can make sure everyone wins.

Do pay attention to total pricing. Sometimes Performers get so excited about a purchase that they overshoot their budget – sometimes by a lot. Now, the budget is not necessarily your concern, but earning a lifelong customer *is* your concern – so don't pile anything on if it seems irresponsible. This is a tricky line to walk; there are many people out there who save money on some areas, so they can focus their spending on what they love – whether it's audio, the outdoors, off-roading, photography, or various forms of collecting.

INVITING DIRECTORS

· ·

Present your Invitation deferentially. Do not communicate as the expert speaking from on high – ask for the Director's approval for your recommendation.

"So, based on what I think you're looking for – and please tell me if I seem off base here…"

"I think we have a model that would fit your needs – would you mind if I showed it to you and you can let me know what you think of it?"

"We've had a few customers with similar requirements, and we have a model that quite a few of them have picked out – I'd like to show it to you and see what you think. Would you like to see it?"

Of course, there are some concerns to keep in mind – mostly concerning how we may react to a Director.

I'm not letting them drive the bus! Those of us who use the Director mode most of the time ourselves will be very uncomfortable taking this seemingly subservient position. (I know it was difficult for me to use at first.) Of course we have some responsibility for the results, , but my final reply to this concern is really, "Too bad – deal with it." Our desires to look smart, capable, and well-informed are less important than assisting customers to make the right purchase. If this is what it takes to follow the Fourth Rule, why not?

If this is good enough for everyone else, it's good enough for them! You may have the single most popular item in the history of your category – the Director doesn't care. Directors are perfectly capable of believing that everybody else has goofed up – but that they will make the right choice.

They may be the boss in their own field, but I'm the expert here, so they should listen to me! Maybe they should. So what? You may know exactly what the Director should be buying. The best way to prevent the Director from buying that item is to tell the Director what to do. You can rail against the weather, but it doesn't change as a result – and neither will our customers. Follow the Fourth Rule and decide that winning in this case means winning the business.

INVITING CARETAKERS

· ·

Caretakers are easy to sell things to. They often buy what you want them to buy, instead of what they really want (or would want if they knew more about the category). With Caretakers, it's critical to not abuse their trust and sell them more than what serves them. You lose them forever as a customer if you do that – and they may return or cancel it after their Director spouse, brother, parent, or friend learns about it..

Often, Caretakers who have been taken advantage of in the past go shopping with a minder - often a Director or Researcher whose job is to keep them out of trouble. For this reason, working with a Caretaker client often involves presenting to more than one person, and the second person often uses a different Pattern. Now, you're selling to two people, and the respectful path is to keep both in mind – don't drop the Caretaker so you can focus on their "minder," because the disrespect is apparent, and you will probably lose the buying group completely.

Present to your entire audience.

I have a friend who used to represent a premium medical-supply company. We went out to lunch, and when I returned to the store, he watched me help a two-person buying group looking for a radio. While neither of these two ladies were car-stereo experts, one was quite obviously a Caretaker, and the other was quite obviously her Director friend brought along to keep the Caretaker from being taken advantage of. Once I realized that the buyer wasn't in charge, her friend was, I presented to them both - but in a way that acknowledged that they were in charge, and I was not. At one point, to demonstrate the radio (which was at the bottom of our display board), I got down on one knee and looked up at both of them as I demonstrated its functions. I avoided jockeying for position with the Director - I deferred to her very clearly - and so I made the sale.

My lunch friend told me afterward that he couldn't hear the conversation, but the body language had been fascinating to watch. Because his sales presentations often involved multiple people serving in different roles, he found the entire interaction to be very educational. Present to your *entire* audience.

INVITING RESEARCHERS

Researchers are the toughest clients to win over, and I absolutely love working with them *because I finally learned what they need!* They care a lot, and they don't expect anyone else to care as much as they do. Once they find out I care a lot too, they're clients for life.

Many accountants and engineers use the Researcher Pattern often. It's a great skill for people in those fields to have in their toolbox.

First off, they need time. They will rarely make a decision on my timetable. My wife uses the Researcher Pattern often – she's a CPA with a specialty in specific tax matters – and for many years, people have been trying to get her to decide quickly where to go for lunch. It's not going to happen. She won't make a decision until she goes through her process.

Secondly, they need to do their own research. That's fine – as long as they aren't doing that research on my time, of course. I often need to do my own research to make a compelling presentation.

So, I transition from the initial mode of contact to email as quickly as possible (no matter how they contact me, I transition to email – even if they visit my showroom, I rarely try to "close a deal" with a Researcher on the first visit), and in that email message, I use my version of General Colin Powell's doctrine of "overwhelming force." I send a message that explains who I am and who my company is, what problems I see that we will need to overcome, and how I plan to overcome them. I apologize up front for the length of the email, I stipulate that it may take a few times to reread it, and I state that there will probably be questions that arise and that I'm happy to answer them. If the client is using the Researcher Pattern, they love communication with a lot of data. It really sets you apart from others.

Make sure the message is well-written and properly punctuated. One way I do this is by reusing content over and over. There are many services now, such as Grammarly, which can help folks with well-composed content.

Include high-quality pictures. Researchers love to read, but all humans find visual communication powerful.

When it's time to make a recommendation, provide three choices. As I was proposing projects, I included a fairly detailed proposal that focused on the amount of time each granular task would require and rolled up the total time into a dollar amount. People love to debate what an item costs, but few people want to debate what time a task requires. If you're simply presenting options without a task component, the triplicate of choice is still very powerful. I always use the lowest-cost option as my last resort if price is a big deal, the middle option is one I really want the client to select, and the third option is where I swing for the fences and offer something really cool - and sometimes extreme.

Discuss value as well as price, but keep price in mind. Researchers would often let me know they found an item cheaper somewhere else (and it was always on the internet). I would reply that this wasn't surprising – that's pretty much what the internet is for, and if items weren't cheaper on the internet, nothing would ever sell on the internet due to the poor customer service experience. Researchers are often a bit taken aback that I wasn't that worried about price, but I rarely ended up having to make any price concessions! Making the value clear helps you keep the deal in the face of price competition, and it also often keeps you from having to move on price at all.

STEP FOUR: THE IMPLEMENTATION

The purpose of the Implementation is to earn the business we've sold.

This is the part where the client gets the product or service; has it installed, delivered, or put through the activation process; and uses it for the first time. To do that, they have to:

- Decide to buy it
- Pay for it
- Fill out some paperwork or sign up
- Have it installed
- Get some explanation on how to use it

At that point, you have to actually deliver on your promises. This provides a great corrective-feedback loop – if a salesperson isn't involved with the Implementation, mistakes can be repeated over and over. This experience changes who we are and makes us more effective salespeople with future clients.

There are many tricky moments in the Implementation stage. In small businesses, the salesperson is often the project manager as well, and there is a beautiful symmetry to this. It's rare to find a great salesperson who is a great project manager – that person is a great white elk. On the other hand, a great project manager can become a really good salesperson, and really good is better than what most business plans call for.

In modern B2B selling, the salesperson is often removed from this process, and I think that's a mistake. They may not be the project manager of a big Implementation, but they should be in the loop. Their ability to sell can only improve if they have more real-world experience with the company's offering.

CONCLUDING THE FOUR STEPS

1. **Introduction**
2. **Investigation**
3. **Invitation**
4. **Implementation**

Follow this sequence, and everything will get easier.

PUTTING IT ALL TOGETHER

So, what have we learned?

We can pursue sales ethically – and stress is the result of ignoring this truth and acting unethically.

Selling has a simple progression – and stress results from ignoring that simple progression.

Variations in people's unconscious tendencies make selling more complex – treating everyone the same doesn't work and leads to stressful interaction.

How do we start?

Start with the Rules. This shouldn't take too long. The Rules basically boil down to, "Be a good person who contributes." The section on Rules exists to keep us from going over to the dark side of selling, and helps us sustain those relationships.

Follow the Steps. The Steps are what you start off memorizing – along with the tips on language and body language to follow as you go through the Steps. Remember to invite, and then stop talking - and to use the WADE formula when applicable.

Rise above your Pattern. We can't say this enough – start with your Pattern, not the client's Pattern! Put your oxygen mask on first. If you don't identify your Patterns, take responsibility for them, and navigate them consciously, identifying the Patterns of others isn't very useful. Understanding your Primary Pattern, and its strengths and weaknesses in selling, will give you tips on how to work with all your potential customers in the most effective way possible.

Do the work, practice, and create satisfaction - sustainably!